of years to reach Earth. Some of the distant objects Hubble has photographed may no longer even exist. Hubble revealed how stars form, age and eventually die, expanding massively into red giants before finally running out of energy and cooling. Astronomers have even seen circles of dust collecting around stars. The dust will eventually clump together to form planets. With Hubble, we can watch the history of our own solar system played out in other planetary systems far away.

Visiting the stars without leaving Earth

Since the moon missions in the 1960s, humans have not ventured outside Earth's orbit, but unmanned probes have gone much further afield. In 1990, the probe Magellan began sending back images of Venus from its mission to map the planet. In 2004, the Mars Exploration Rovers began their exploration of Mars, taking photographs and collecting and analysing samples of rock and dust.

This photo is one of many taken by the Hubble Space Telescope, offering astronomers fascinating new insights into the cosmos. This shows the Omega or Swan Nebula, an area where new stars are formed, some 5,500 light years from Earth in the constellation Sagittarius.

⊙ eye witness

Every image taken will be an image not of the universe as it is now, but as it was at, say, half its present age — before the solar system was formed. You're really going far back in time to understand the evolutionary processes by which the universe got to its present state. So many better questions are being asked now than 25 years ago ... and with machines such as the space telescope we can actually begin to hope to get answers.

Professor Malcolm Longair, the Astronomer Royal for Scotland, 1990

- **FURTHER INFORMATION**
  📖 Books:
  Eye on the Universe: The Incredible Hubble Space Telescope
  by Michael D Cole (Enslow Publishers, 2012)
  🖱 Websites:
  hubblesite.org/
  Hubble's official website

Iraq Invades Kuwait

The people of the small Gulf state of Kuwait slept peacefully in the early hours of 2 August 1990, unaware that their country was being invaded. Over 100,000 troops and 700 tanks from neighbouring Iraq crossed the border and quickly took control. The emir, the leader of Kuwait, escaped immediately into Saudi Arabia, a country friendly towards Western nations such as the United States and Britain. The Iraqi leader, Saddam Hussein, threatened to turn the country's capital, Kuwait City, into a graveyard if other nations tried to stop his army.

Events quickly escalated. Foreign powers decided it was important to liberate Kuwait and protect neighbouring Saudi Arabia. US troops began to arrive within days of the invasion to protect the border of Saudi Arabia in an operation called Desert Shield. The Security Council of the United Nations imposed economic sanctions on Iraq and demanded that the country withdraw its troops from Kuwait. Led by the United States and Britain, a coalition of forces from 34 countries closed in on Iraq.

US Marines prepare to blow up a portrait of Iraqi leader Saddam Hussein in Al Jahrah, north-western Kuwait.

Oil and land

Kuwait had originally been part of Basra, an area of Iraq, but became a separate territory in 1922. Iraq finally accepted Kuwait's independence in 1963, but the two nations continued to dispute their border. For Iraq, there was more at stake than land. Both Iraq and Kuwait had become wealthy from selling oil to the rest of the world. Iraq claimed that Kuwait was selling too much oil, pushing down the price, and even taking some of it from

Contents

GLOBAL EVENTS

BRITISH EVENTS

The Hubble Space Telescope is Launched

Seventy years after a telescope in space was first suggested, the shuttle Discovery blasted into space carrying the Hubble Space Telescope. It had been built as a joint project by NASA and the European Space Agency (ESA). The size of a school bus, the telescope was positioned in orbit above the Earth. From there it would collect the clearest pictures ever seen of distant stars and galaxies. Scientists from all over the world booked time with Hubble to assist them in their projects. It quickly became a valuable tool for science everywhere.

The Hubble Space Telescope is retrieved by the Space Shuttle Endeavour so that astronauts can carry out repairs.

Light from the stars is processed by instruments on board Hubble. Information and images are sent by radio link to Earth. The same link is used to control the telescope. Expected to stay in space until 2013, Hubble is serviced, repaired and improved by astronauts and robots. This was put to the test early on: a tiny manufacturing fault in one of Hubble's mirrors had to be corrected by astronauts in 1993 before Hubble could send back crystal-clear images.

Staring into space

The world was soon stunned by the astonishing photographs from Hubble. For the first time, astronomers could see detailed images of galaxies unimaginable distances from Earth. The images from Hubble are ten times clearer than anything that can be seen from the ground, since Earth's atmosphere absorbs, reflects and distorts light from space. Images of distant objects are also images from distant times. The light from other galaxies has taken millions or billions

Iraqi oil fields. Low oil prices hit Iraq hard. Saddam Hussein believed the United States would not interfere in an invasion of Kuwait. He was wrong. The US led the assault on the occupying Iraqi forces.

All-out war

The deadline for withdrawal ended on 15 January 1991, yet Iraqi forces continued to occupy Kuwait. Two days later, the coalition forces launched the longest air strike in military history. Called Desert Storm, the assault targeted Iraqi troops and installations in Kuwait, and military and civilian targets inside Iraq. Iraq launched missiles against Israel and Saudi Arabia, both states with strong ties to the West.

The war lasted six weeks. Defeat came for Iraq at the end of February 1991. As Iraqi troops retreated from Kuwait City on the night of 26-27 February, US fighter planes bombed them continuously. The road from the city became known as the Highway of Death. Although Iraq called for a ceasefire, no formal peace agreement was ever reached, leaving the way open for future conflict.

Highway of Death: as Iraqi military personnel and their families fled Kuwait, they came under air assault from coalition forces. The attack left hundreds of destroyed vehicles littering the highway from Kuwait to Iraq.

eye witness

My wife and children were shocked at the destruction that was so close to our house, now they could understand all the shelling, booming and rattling of windows for two days and most importantly why they had to remain away from windows. As we rode in, almost every official Kuwait government building along the route had been shelled, torched, or destroyed. Wrecked and smoldering vehicles littered the highway some with the charred remains present. The once well manicured and green medians were now brown, dried up and trashed.

LTC Fred L Hart, Jr, a US military adviser to the Kuwaiti Land Forces, who witnessed the Iraqi invasion

- **SEE ALSO**
Pages 14–15: 13 September 1993
Peace in the Middle East?

- **FURTHER INFORMATION**
  Books:
  The Persian Gulf War by Josh Gregory (Children's Press, 2011)
  The Gulf War by Suzanne J Murdico (Rosen Publishing Group, 2004)
  Websites:
  www.pbs.org/wgbh/pages/frontline/gulf/
  Chronology of the invasion and subsequent war

Eruption of Mount Pinatubo

On 15 June 1991 a massive eruption blew away the summit of the volcano Pinatubo, devastating the island of Luzon in the Philippines. A column of scorching ash, gases and lava (molten rock) blasted 34 kilometres into the air. The eruption hurled ash and lava over an area of 125,000 square kilometres. Searing winds rushed from the volcano, destroying everything in their path. Ash lay five centimetres deep around the volcano and even fell as far away as Cambodia and Vietnam. It was the second largest eruption of the century, and killed 300 people.

At the same time, a tropical storm struck the island. The howling wind and torrential rain combined with the falling ash to make deadly mud flows called lahars, which can travel at up to 65 kilometres per hour. Most of the people who died were crushed by roofs collapsing under the weight of wet ash.

A sleeping giant wakes

Pinatubo had lain dormant for 500 years and the 30,000 people living on its forested slopes had no idea their homes were on a volcano until 1990. After an earthquake on 16 July struck the centre of the island, a series of small earthquakes and eruptions signalled that the volcano was waking up. Activity increased in the spring and early summer of 1991

A giant mushroom cloud of volcanic ash rises over Mount Pinatubo.

Five months after the eruption of Mount Pinatubo, Santa Barbara Elementary School on Luzon still lies buried up to its roof in volcanic ash. The eruption caused widespread damage to buildings and infrastructure and left 250,000 people homeless.

and became much more violent in early June, with eruptions of lava and ash. By 14 June, 60,000 people had left the area around the volcano and 18,000 had left a nearby air base.

Lasting effects

The final eruption threw so much ash, dust and gas into the atmosphere that global temperatures dropped by about 0.5°C and took two years to recover. Five years later, whole valleys on Luzon were still filled with deep piles of ash, some of it as hot as 500°C. It could stay scorching hot for decades. Lahars are still occurring, and have destroyed 100,000 homes. The sloppy volcanic mud forms into huge lakes. When the sediment settles, the water eventually breaks out without warning and the flood causes another lahar.

A decade of disasters

Mount Unzen, in Japan, erupted a week before Pinatubo, killing 35 people. A series of devastating earthquakes shook the world in the 1990s, too. Iran suffered its worst-ever natural disaster on 17 June 1990 when an earthquake killed 50,000 people and injured 100,000. Earthquakes in India on 30 September 1993 killed up to 22,000 people, and on 17 January 1995 the largest earthquake to strike Japan in more than 70 years killed 6,432 people in Kobe.

What the papers said

The greatest threats to human lives may come from overlooked, long dormant volcanoes. To monitor a volcano requires identifying it beforehand; as recently as 1981, Pinatubo was not even included in the worldwide registry of volcanoes maintained by the Smithsonian Institution. "When a nice little hill covered with lush vegetation finally wakes up," observes Smithsonian volcanologist Tom Simkin, "it's going to cause a lot of damage."

Time, 24 June 1991

- **SEE ALSO**
  Pages 24–25: 6 May 1995
  Ebola Fever Strikes in Africa

- **FURTHER INFORMATION**
  📖 Books:
  Eyewitness: Volcano by Susanna van Rose
  (Dorling Kindersley, 2011)
  🖱 Websites:
  park.org/Philippines/pinatubo/index.html
  An account of the eruption

The World Wide Web Goes Live

The first click on hyperlinked text to go from one page to another over the Internet happened in Switzerland on 6 August 1991. The World Wide Web began at that moment. Over a few short years it would grow into a global network of shared information on every imaginable topic.

The invention was the work of Tim Berners-Lee, a British researcher at the CERN laboratory in Geneva, Switzerland. He had set out to help physics researchers at CERN to share their work seamlessly by linking their papers together on a network of computers. But he soon realised the concept could be extended to any information, anywhere in the world, by using the Internet to move the information around. (The Internet itself had existed since 1969, when it began as ARPANET, a network created for the US Defence department.)

In early 1991, physics departments in a number of European universities shared the first web pages on a private network. In August 1991 Berners-Lee released his invention to the world using the Internet. The first web page had the address info.cern.ch/hypertext/WWW/TheProject.html. But just a single web server was no use. The Web depended on other people putting up their own websites and linking them together.

⊙ eye witness

In August I released three things – the *WorldWideWeb* for NeXT, the line-mode browser, and the basic server for any machine – outside CERN by making them all available on the Internet. I posted a notice on several Internet newsgroups, chief among them alt.hypertext…. Putting the Web out on alt.hypertext was a watershed event. It exposed the Web to a very critical academic community. I began to get e-mail from people…. 'Hey, I've just set up a server, and it's dead cool. Here's the address.'

Tim Berners-Lee, *Weaving the Web* (Orion Business Books, 1999)

Up and running – fast

Berners-Lee developed tools other people could use to make and view web pages. A physics laboratory in Stanford, California, set up the first web server outside Europe. By November 1992, there were 26 servers in the world. A year later there were more than 200. Berners-Lee invited other people to produce software for the Web. The Mosaic browser, developed in 1993, proved popular. It would eventually turn into Internet Explorer. With good browsers for

*Robert Cailliau (left) with
the original NeXT computer terminal on
which the World Wide Web was created. Calliau
worked with Berners-Lee on the project.*

popular PC and Macintosh computers the Web took off rapidly. By the
end of 1993 there were at least 500 web servers. By the end of 1994 there
were 10,000, and ten million users.

Changing face of the Web

The very first web pages were nothing like modern web pages.
Pages could not yet mix text and pictures. There were no
sound, video, animations or fancy text designs. But
as more people started to use the Web, it rapidly
evolved and more features appeared. Private
individuals started using the Web, and even
buying computers just so they could use it. Soon,
people were using the Web for business, education,
entertainment, personal communication and
shopping. Within a single decade the existence of
the World Wide Web transformed business and
social life around the world.

- **SEE ALSO**
  Pages 4–5: 24 April 1990
  The Hubble Space Telescope is Launched
  Pages 20–21: 6 May 1994
  The Channel Tunnel Opens
  Pages 30–31: 5 July 1996
  Dolly the Sheep is Born

- **FURTHER INFORMATION**
  Books:
  Tim Berners-Lee: Inventor of the World Wide Web
  by Stephanie Sammartino McPherson
  (Tewnty-First Century Books, 2009)
  Websites:
  news.bbc.co.uk/1/hi/technology/5242252.stm
  How the Web went worldwide

The End of the Soviet Union

The Soviet Union finally came to a peaceful end on 8 December 1991. The communist state had been in severe decline for most of the 1980s. Its state-run economy was very inefficient. Also, the Soviet Union could no longer compete with the United States, its main military rival. Mikhail Gorbachev (ruled 1985–1991) tried to reform the economy, but his attempt came too late and was poorly managed. He only succeeded in weakening the country even more.

By the late 1980s, several of the republics that made up the Soviet Union began to push for independence. In August 1991 hardline communists tried to overthrow Gorbachev and reverse the changes he had made. The coup failed, but the republics realized that they would be better off as independent states.

On 8 December 1991 the leaders of three republics, Russia, Belarus and the Ukraine, signed the Belavezha Accords, dissolving the Soviet Union. The remaining republics completed the process by signing the Alma-Ata Protocol on 21 December 1991. The 15 newly independent states agreed to form a loose confederation called the Commonwealth of Independent States (CIS).

During the attempted coup of August 1991, Boris Yeltsin stands defiantly in front of the Russian parliament building, refusing to surrender the government to the coup leaders.

Ending 80 years of communism

The Soviet Union was formed in 1922, five years after the overthrow of the tsar in the Russian Revolution. It was a one-party communist state, with power concentrated in the hands of the ruling Communist Party. People were not allowed to own private property and the state controlled the economy and all trade.

After World War II, tension mounted between the Soviet Union and the United States. The Soviet Union took control of Eastern Europe, exercising its authority through communist puppet regimes. The world divided into two hostile camps, one allied to the Soviet Union and the other with the US – a period known as the Cold War. In 1989, Gorbachev ended Soviet control of Eastern Europe. The communist states there swiftly collapsed, ending the Cold War.

After communism

After 1991, Russia, the dominant republic of the former Soviet Union, moved quickly towards a free market economy. The change was not well managed. Prices rose out of control, and basic goods such as food and clothing were in short supply. While a few people grew very wealthy, most Russians had a low standard of living. Corruption and crime were everywhere, with organized gangs running many businesses.

In 1994, the province of Chechnya declared independence from Russia, leading to a war (1994–96) in which 50,000 people died. The newly independent Chechen state was lawless and chaotic, and war broke out again in 1999–2000.

Hard times in post-communist Russia: a homeless woman and child huddle under a ledge on Nevsky Prospekt in the city of St Petersburg.

What the papers said

The Soviet Union died after a long illness which took a decisive turn for the worse some time during 1989. The moment of death went unnoticed because of the massacre of its Eastern European relatives. We are left with a zombie. It makes little sense to rejoice in dismembering it, particularly into parts that still have the power of regeneration.

Sunday Times, 8 December 1991

• **SEE ALSO**
Pages 26–27: 12 July 1995
Massacre at Srebrenica

• **FURTHER INFORMATION**
📖 Books:
Years of Russia, the USSR and the Collapse of Soviet Communism
by Jane Jenkins (Hodder Education, 2008)
Websites:
news.bbc.co.uk/onthisday/hi/dates/stories/december/25/newsid_2542000/2542749.stm
Gorbachev's resignation and the break-up of the Soviet Union

Peace in the Middle East?

Peace in the Middle East finally looked possible with the signing of the Oslo Accords on the lawn of the White House in Washington, DC. Since Israel was established in 1948, the Jewish state had been in conflict with the Arab world. The Accords were agreed in Oslo, Norway, on 20 August 1993 and signed in the United States a month later by Yasser Arafat, leader of the Palestine Liberation Organisation (PLO), and Yitzhak Rabin, prime minister of Israel.

Ancient claims

Traditionally, the Jewish people have felt a sacred attachment to the land now occupied by Israel. It had been a Jewish kingdom in Biblical times, and Jews believe the land was promised to them by God. From the late 19th century, Jews escaping persecution in Russia and Europe began settling the land. By then it was known as Palestine and was part of the Turkish Ottoman Empire. As the numbers of Jewish settlers grew, they came into increasing conflict with the Arab Muslims (Palestinians) living there.

Establishment of Israel

At the end of World War I, the Ottoman Empire collapsed and Britain took charge of Palestine. In the 1930s growing numbers of Jews arrived, many fleeing from rising anti-Jewish feelings in

US president Bill Clinton brings Israeli prime minister Yitzhak Rabin (left) and PLO chairman Yasser Arafat together for a historic handshake.

⊙ eye witness

The horizons to peace are open. There is a stirring in the entire Arab arena in their readiness to make peace. Not that there aren't obstacles, not that there aren't difficulties. But I'm convinced that the horizons to peace are open.

Yitzhak Rabin, in a speech to the Israeli parliament, 1993

Europe, especially after Hitler's rise to power in 1933. The British rulers struggled to control the increasing violence between Jewish settlers and Palestinians. Britain decided to give up its mandate in 1947. The United Nations planned to divide Palestine into two states, one Jewish, one Arab, with Jerusalem an international city. The Jewish community accepted the plan; the Palesinians did not. When Israel was founded in May 1948, the neighbouring Arab states immediately declared war. By 1949, Israel had triumphed.

Continuing conflict: a Jewish settler fires warning shots after Palestinians set fire to a construction site near the settlement of Beit El on the West Bank in August 1995.

Palestinian-Israeli conflict

In 1967 Israel won another war and occupied additional territories, including the Gaza Strip and the West Bank (known thereafter as the Occupied Territories). After 1967, the PLO rose to the forefront of the Palestinian struggle. The PLO frequently used terrorism as a means of pursuing its aims. The conflict continued, with few opportunities for peace, until the 1990s.

Towards peace

The Oslo Accords represented a breakthrough. For the first time Palestinians acknowledged the right of Israel to exist. The parties also agreed to the creation of a Palestine National Authority, with civil (though not military) authority over parts of the Occupied Territories. Israel and the PLO agreed to resolve their remaining differences through negotiation, not armed conflict. These included the status of Jerusalem, Jewish settlements in the Occupied Territories and the right of Palestinian refugees to return to Israel.

Despite a promising start, the Oslo Accords did not provide an easy path to peace. During the later 1990s, terrorist attacks by Palestinian groups such as Hamas eroded support for the peace process in Israel. Jewish settlements continued to be built in the Occupied Territories, inflaming Arab opinion. A renewed attempt to reach peace in 2000 failed.

- **SEE ALSO**
Pages 6–7: 2 August 1990
Iraq Invades Kuwait

- **FURTHER INFORMATION**
  📖 Books:
  The Arab-Israeli War Since 1948
  by Alex Woolf (Heinemann Library, 2012)
  🖱 Websites:
  news.bbc.co.uk/cbbcnews/hi/newsid_1600000/newsid_1602700/1602748.stm
  A guide to the Israeli-Palestinian conflict

Genocide in Rwanda

When unknown killers shot down a plane carrying two African presidents, it sparked violence that quickly turned into genocide. The world stood by while 800,000 people were butchered. The two presidents were Juvénal Habyarimana of Rwanda, a small state in Central Africa, and Cyprien Ntaryamira of neighbouring Burundi. They were on their way home from peace talks between representatives of the rival Tutsi and Hutu tribes. Their journey ended anything but peacefully. Both men were members of the Hutu tribe. The Hutus assumed a Tutsi had shot down their plane, and they launched a pitiless assault on the Tutsis in Rwanda.

Two tribes

Rwanda and Burundi had once been a single country, ruled by Belgium and home to both Hutus and Tutsis. The Belgians favoured the Tutsis over the Hutus, causing tension between the groups. When the Hutus rioted and killed 20,000 Tutsis in 1959, Belgium withdrew and two new countries were formed. Most Hutus settled in Rwanda, and most Tutsis in Burundi.

A group of Tutsis in Uganda wanted to overthrow Habyarimana and return to Rwanda. They formed the Rwandan Patriotic Front (RPF). In Rwanda, Habyarimana persecuted the Tutsis, accusing them of being RPF sympathizers. He made peace with the RPF in August 1993, but when he was assassinated, the Hutus blamed the Tutsis and turned on them.

A child looks at the remains of some 25,000 Tutsis, and some Hutus, who were massacred in and around the Nyamata Catholic church and in the surrounding Kanzenze community in Rwanda.

Massacre

Within hours, the presidential guard murdered opposition political leaders and sent troops to slaughter Tutsis throughout the country. An unofficial Hutu group, the Interahamwe, swept through the country murdering, raping and mutilating Tutsis. Police and soldiers led the slaughter, but ordinary citizens were

Some of the 250,000 Rwandan refugees that crossed the border into Tanzania, following the massacre.

quickly recruited or forced to join in. At its height, the Interahamwe had 30,000 members. Over a period of 100 days, they killed 800,000 Tutsis.

The international community did nothing to prevent the massacre. UN forces withdrew after ten UN soldiers died. In July, the RPF captured the capital, Kigali, and imposed a ceasefire. Terrified that they would now suffer in turn, two million Hutus fled the country. They poured into neighbouring Zaire (now the Democratic Republic of Congo), causing a humanitarian crisis – there was nowhere for them to go but refugee camps with insufficient food and no medical aid. In July, a new government, with a Hutu president and many RPF ministers, promised a safe return for all refugees.

Investigations continued for years after the massacre. Ten years later, 100,000 people were still in prison and 500 had been executed for their parts in the massacre. However, many of the massacre's ringleaders escaped justice.

⊙ eye witness

People were sliced to pieces with machetes and axes, skulls crushed with rocks and children tied in sacks and tossed into rivers…. In the banana fields there are more dead bodies than bananas. This can only be compared to what the Nazis did.

Anonymous witness to the massacre

- **SEE ALSO**
  Pages 18–19: 27 April 1994
  Black Rule in South Africa
  Pages 26–27: 12 July 1995
  Massacre at Srebrenica

- **FURTHER INFORMATION**
  📖 Books:
  The Rwanda Genocide
  by Dan Nardo
  (Lucent Books, 2011)
  The Rwanda Genocide
  by Christina Fisanick
  (Greenhaven Press, 2004)
  Websites:
  www.bbc.co.uk/news/world-africa-14093238
  Rwanda country profile

Black Rule in South Africa

Joyful scenes greeted the election of Nelson Mandela as the first black president of South Africa on 27 April 1994. After 27 years in jail, Mandela was finally freed in 1990. With the first free elections in South Africa's history, Mandela now saw his dream of freedom for black people come true. His election as president ended more than a century of unfair treatment of the black majority by the white minority in South Africa. The African National Congress party (ANC), which Mandela led, won 252 of the 400 seats in the South African parliament.

Apartheid

The position of black people in South Africa had turned around completely in less than a decade. Since the birth of South Africa in 1910, the white population, of European descent, had oppressed the black majority. This racial discrimination became formalized in 1948 when the National Party introduced a system known as apartheid, which forced black and white people to live and work apart. From the 1960s, black people were made to move into 'homelands' and townships, poor shanty towns on the outskirts of the more prosperous cities. Black people had few rights and were not considered citizens of South Africa.

The ANC campaigned peacefully at first, and then more violently, against apartheid. The government outlawed the ANC and Mandela was imprisoned for life in 1962. In jail, he became the figurehead of the movement to end apartheid, supported around the world.

By the end of the 1980s, the combined pressures of internal rebellion and international isolation finally forced the South African government to make concessions. In 1989, the ban on the ANC was lifted, and in 1990 Mandela was freed. He worked with the South African president F W de Klerk to dismantle the apartheid system and establish South Africa as a multiracial democracy. They achieved that goal with the elections of 1994. Mandela and De Klerk were jointly awarded the Nobel Prize for Peace in 1993.

⊙ eye witness

Let there be justice for all.
Let there be peace for all.
Let there be work, bread, water and salt for all.
Let each know that for each the body, the mind and the soul have been freed to fulfil themselves.
Never, never and never again shall it be that this beautiful land will again experience the oppression of one by another and suffer the indignity of being the skunk of the world.

Nelson Mandela, 10 May 1994

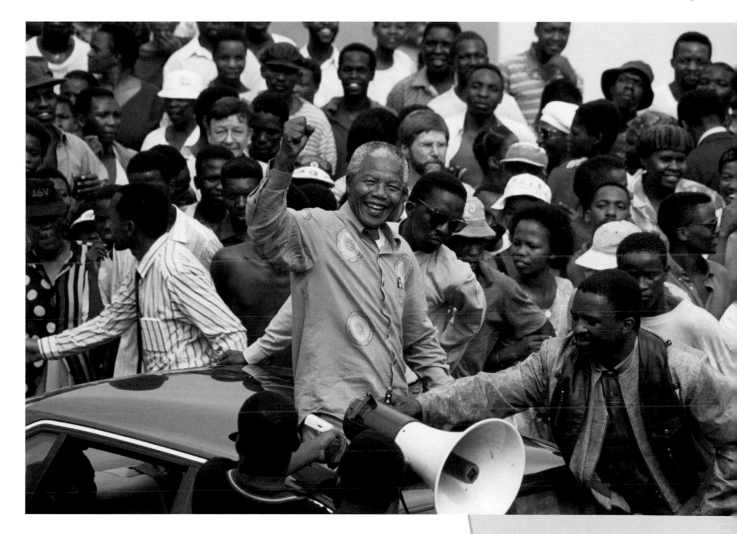

Former political prisoner Nelson Mandela campaigns for the presidency of South Africa.

A difficult path

Winning the election was a huge step forward for South Africa, but the country still had to deal with the legacy of its violent and divided past. Under the leadership of Bishop Desmond Tutu, the Truth and Reconciliation Commission set about investigating and acknowledging the terrible things that had happened in the recent past. They intended not to blame or punish people, but bring events out into the open and enable the country to move on from a position of honesty.

South Africa also faced other difficulties. The years of apartheid had caused a vast rich–poor divide. The new government had to struggle with the poverty suffered by most of the black population, the terrible housing shortage and the squalor of the townships. The country was also ravaged by HIV/Aids. These challenges continued into the 21st century.

- **SEE ALSO**
Pages 16–17: 6 April 1994
Genocide in Rwanda
Pages 32–33: 1 July 1997
Hong Kong Returns to China

- **FURTHER INFORMATION**
  📖 Books:
  The End of Apartheid in South Africa
  by Liz Sonneborn
  (Chelsea House Publishers, 2010)
  🖰 Websites:
  www.pbs.org/wgbh/pages/frontline/shows/mandela/
  Mandela's life and triumph.

The Channel Tunnel Opens

On 6 May 1994 it became possible to travel from England to France without crossing water for the first time since the end of the last ice age, nearly 10,000 years ago. That day saw the opening of the Channel Tunnel, a rail tunnel beneath the English Channel, the sea between England and France. It allows trains to travel between London and Paris in just over two hours. Other trains, called Le Shuttle, carry road vehicles under the Channel between Kent and northern France in only 35 minutes.

The dream of a tunnel beneath the Channel began in 1802 when Albert Mathieu-Favier suggested a tunnel for horse-drawn carriages, lit by oil lamps. In 1875 both the British and French governments gave the go-ahead to build a tunnel, but the money was not available. Building stopped and started several times between 1922 and 1975, until the idea was relaunched in 1984. A formal treaty was signed on 12 February 1986, and work began in 1988.

6 May 1994: the Eurostar Channel Tunnel train pulls out of the international terminal at Waterloo Station on its first journey.

What the media said

The Queen embarked on today's historic journey from the new Channel Tunnel terminal in London's Waterloo Station accompanied by much of her government and other leading British politicians. Her Majesty was to travel in the new Eurostar passenger train along the first land link between Britain and the Continent since the Ice Age.... With a full commercial service still perhaps nine months away, serious doubts hang over its long-term financial viability.

Mike Smart, BBC News, 6 May 1994

French and English workers shake hands after a giant drilling machine broke through the last section of ground separating the English and French halves of the Channel Tunnel.

A major feat of engineering

The Channel Tunnel is 50 kilometres long. It is the third longest tunnel in the world and is the longest undersea tunnel. The Channel Tunnel is actually three tunnels running side by side. One carries trains from France to England, another carries trains from England to France, and a service tunnel runs between them. It took 30,000 construction workers seven years to complete the tunnel. Most of it is 40 metres under the sea bed. It was started from both ends, using laser surveying tools to make sure the two tunnels were lined up. When they met, the centre lines of the two tunnels were out of alignment by only 358 millimetres horizontally and 58 millimetres vertically.

Unwelcome guests

When the Channel Tunnel first opened, some people in Britain worried that the disease rabies would spread from Europe to Britain, carried through the service tunnel by animals. Britain is rabies-free, so electrified grids, tracking and security measures were used to stop wildlife entering the tunnel from France. As rabies control in Europe has improved, the barriers have been removed.

In 1999, the Sangatte refugee camp opened near Calais. Many refugees escaped from the camp and tried to get into Britain illegally by hiding on freight trains heading for Britain through the Channel Tunnel. Several suffered injuries or died attempting to jump onto trains. The camp was closed in 2002.

SEE ALSO
Pages 10–11: 6 August 1991
The World Wide Web Goes Live
Pages 30–31: 5 July 1996
Dolly the Sheep is Born

FURTHER INFORMATION
Books:
The Chunnel by Marcia Amidon Lusted (Lucent Books, 2005)
Websites:
www.theotherside.co.uk/tm-heritage/background/tunnel.htm
A history of the Channel Tunnel from the first plans

Nerve Gas Attack on the Tokyo Underground

People fled from the Tokyo underground system and collapsed as a deadly nerve gas spread through five stations during the early morning rush hour. The sarin gas was released by members of the religious group Aum Shinrikyo ('Supreme Truth') in the most serious assault in Japan since World War II. Twelve people died and 50 were seriously injured. Five thousand have suffered lasting health problems.

Each member of the group had a bag of sarin wrapped in newspaper. At a pre-arranged time, they each dropped a bag on the floor and punctured it with a sharpened umbrella. The sarin liquid evaporated and spread as a gas, breathed in by people nearby. Altogether, the group used a litre of sarin. A single drop the size of a pinhead is enough to kill an adult.

Panic – and good fortune

At first, no one knew why the people pouring out of the stations were so ill. The cause was discovered by chance. A doctor who had helped victims of a previous sarin attack on a town outside Tokyo saw the news coverage on television and recognized the symptoms. He contacted the hospital in Tokyo where most of the victims had been taken and told them that sarin poisoning was the cause.

A commuter crouches on a subway platform beside a victim of the sarin gas attack. The gas was released on three different lines of the Tokyo metro during the morning rush hour.

Sarin is a nerve toxin. It interrupts messages going to and from the brain. Victims have disturbed vision and breathing difficulties. They eventually die of suffocation.

As panic spread, many people who were unaffected went to hospitals demanding to be checked. These 'worried well' clogged the hospitals, making it more difficult for medical workers to identify and treat those who were genuinely ill. The incident highlighted problems in emergency planning in Tokyo.

Aum Shinrikyo

Aum Shinrikyo is a religious sect with links to the criminal underworld, including the Japanese mafia, Yakuza. Leaders of Aum taught that the end of the world was approaching and only members of Aum Shinrikyo would survive. The group turned to violence after failing to win seats in the 1989 elections in Japan.

Police raided Aum Shinrikyo premises after the attack and found a massive chemical weapons factory. The group had even sent a team to Zaire in 1994 to collect samples of Ebola, which they hoped to use as a weapon. An earlier attempt to release poison in Tokyo had failed. Twelve members of Aum were sentenced to death for their parts in the Tokyo attacks.

Shoko Asahara, leader of Aum Shinrikyo and mastermind of the 1995 sarin gas attack.

What the papers said

Six people died and more than 1,300 panic-stricken rush-hour commuters were poisoned today as clouds of lethal nerve gas swept through the crowded Tokyo underground network…. As emergency services and hospitals tried to cope with the enormous stream of choking victims, 16 of whom are critical, the shocked Japanese government denounced the atrocity as 'indiscriminate murder'…. With a massive manhunt under way, police revealed that the poison used was Sarin, a nerve gas developed by the Nazis and 20 times more lethal than potassium cyanide.

Evening Standard (London), 20 March 1995

- **SEE ALSO**
  Pages 24–25; 6 May 1995
  Ebola Fever Strikes in Africa
  Pages 36–37: 20 April 1999
  Massacre at Columbine High School

- **FURTHER INFORMATION**
  Books:
  Invisible Weapons: The Science of Biological and Chemical Warfare
  by Don Nardo (Compass Point Books, 2010)
  Websites:
  http://news.bbc.co.uk/1/hi/world/asia-pacific/4365417.stm
  The attack remembered 10 years on, with links to more information

06
MAY
1995

Ebola Fever Strikes in Africa

Panic took hold as information filtered out of Africa: people were dying from a terrible disease in Zaire (now the Democratic Republic of Congo). Victims developed fever and vomiting, then began bleeding from the eyes, mouth, nose and ears. Their internal organs apparently turned to mush and leaked out of their bodies. With no cure or preventive vaccine, people worried that Ebola fever might sweep the world in an unstoppable pandemic. Although Ebola fever did spread rapidly through small communities in Zaire, health authorities managed to bring the outbreak under control within months.

The World Health Organisation (WHO) learned of the outbreak on 6 May 1995. By mid-June, more than 200 people had died from the disease. WHO workers went to Zaire to take over the work of caring for victims and burying the dead. Everyone attending the sick or dealing with dead

In Zaire, everyone had to wear full protective clothing when nursing or burying victims of Ebola fever.

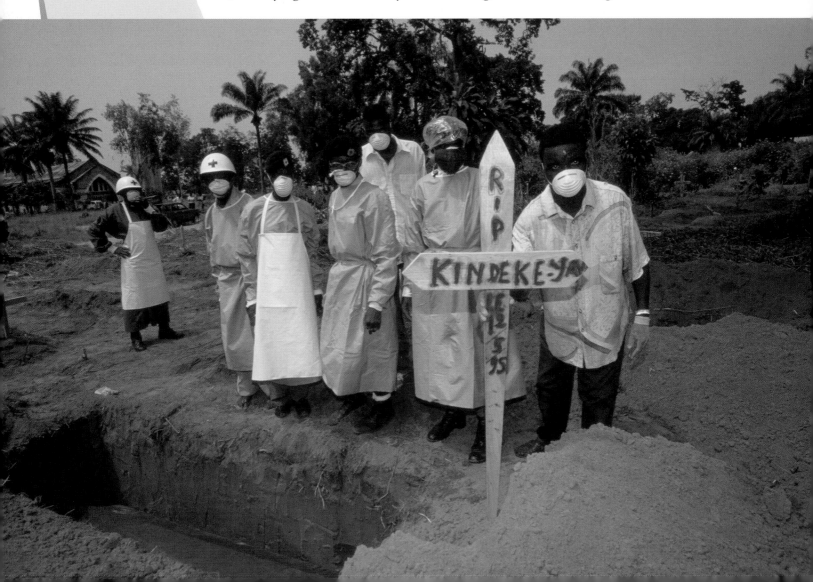

bodies wore full protective clothing, goggles and masks. Many victims of the outbreak were healthcare workers who had treated infected people and had not taken adequate precautions.

Villages were sealed off to prevent people from moving away and possibly carrying the disease with them. These precautions helped to contain the disease and it did not spread further afield. By the end of the outbreak, 250 people had died – eight out of ten of those who caught the disease.

Ebola fever

Ebola fever first appeared in 1976 in an epidemic that killed 431 people. The first signs are fatigue, weakness, headache, backache, vomiting and diarrhoea. These symptoms are followed by a rash, then by bleeding from the intestines, leaking from the mouth and rectum. Victims often also bleed from the ears, nose and eyes. Ebola fever can spread between people, carried in body fluids. There has been some progress towards creating a vaccine to prevent Ebola fever; meanwhile, efforts are focused on controlling outbreaks of the disease as quickly as possible.

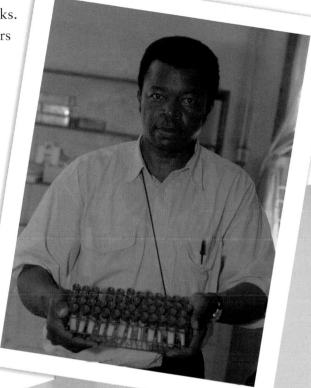

Professor Jean-Jacques Muyembe-Tamfum was the Zairean doctor in charge of the WHO operation during the 1995 Ebola fever epidemic.

What the papers said

Two Italian nuns working in Zaire have died from a jungle disease that turns body organs into liquid…. The Ebola virus has wiped out entire villages in the former Belgian colony and in Sudan and is among the most dangerous known. Some strains can be transmitted in the air, by bite, or by contact with body fluids. They affect virtually every organ in the body, turning tissues into a highly infectious mush.

The Times, 10 May 1995

- **SEE ALSO**
  Pages 16–17: 6 April 1994
  Genocide in Rwanda
  Pages 22–23: 20 March 1995
  Nerve Gas Attack on the Tokyo Underground

- **FURTHER INFORMATION**
- Books:
  Ebola by Aubrey Stimola
  (Rosen Classroom, 2010)
  The Ebola Virus by Kris Hirschmann
  (Lucent, 2006)
- Websites:
  www.bbc.co.uk/radio4/science/ebola.shtml
  Listen to a BBC radio programme about Ebola.

Massacre at Srebrenica

The world was horrified to learn of the slaughter and torture of 8,000 men and boys by Serbian forces at Srebrenica, Bosnia – the worst atrocity on European soil since World War II. On 12 July 1995, Serbian troops began a massacre of 8,000 Bosnian Muslim men and boys. In the refugee camp of Potocari, Serb soldiers separated the men and boys from their families and systematically shot them. In the town, people were randomly shot and tortured, and women were raped. Bodies were pushed into mass graves by bulldozers, and some injured people were buried alive. United Nations (UN) soldiers were present, but were not authorized to use force and were unable to stop the killing. They had to stand by and allow the massacre to take place.

Balkan conflict

There is a long history of ethnic tensions in the Balkans, the region of south-eastern Europe that includes Bosnia. For a long time, Serbia had wanted to be a major force in the region. Serb minorities lived in several surrounding territories, including Bosnia, Croatia, Montenegro and Kosovo. Serb nationalists wished to unite these regions into a 'Greater Serbia', against the will of the non-Serb majorities there.

These tensions were suppressed during the Cold War when the rival states were reorganized as constituent republics of communist Yugoslavia. As communist authority weakened in the late 1980s, several of the republics demanded independence. The Serbian leader, Slobodan Milosevic, wished to keep the republics together under Serbian authority, reviving the idea of a Greater Serbia. Serb forces attacked Croatia in 1991 and Bosnia in 1992 in support of the Serb minorities there who rejected independence.

A little girl and her grieving mother sit close together in a Muslim refugee shelter at Zenica. The girl's father was one of the thousands of Muslims executed by Serbs at Srebrenica.

Ethnic cleansing

In Bosnia, Serb forces drove out Bosnian Muslims from the towns and villages they conquered in order to create new areas for Serbs to live. This process was known as 'ethnic cleansing'. Serb soldiers imprisoned Bosnian Muslim men in concentration camps and raped Bosnian women. The towns the Serbs attacked included some declared 'safe havens' by the UN. One of these was Srebrenica.

NATO steps in

The atrocity at Srebrenica sparked international outrage and spurred the world to belated action. In August 1995 NATO war planes began bombing Serbian troops in Bosnia. Milosevic agreed to peace talks, and the Dayton Accord was signed three weeks later. Milosevic was arrested and put on trial for crimes against humanity at an International War Crimes Tribunal in 2001. He died of a heart attack in 2006 before the end of his trial.

Forensic experts from the International War Crimes Tribunal investigate a mass grave. It contains the remains of some of those killed at Srebrenica.

What the papers said

Nobody has behaved honorably in the face of these atrocities. And there were no real lessons learned from Srebrenica. The same thing happened at the beginning of October around Banja Luka. Men were separated from women and children and taken away. Again the West did nothing, despite knowing about it. There are now 2,000 men missing in that area. There's enough guilt to go around. There's blood on everyone's hands here. You're talking about the biggest European war crime in our lifetime.

Time, 31 October 1995

- **SEE ALSO**

- **FURTHER INFORMATION**
  - 📖 Books:
    Genocide and the Bosnian War
    by Jacqueline Ching
    (Rosen Publishing Group, 2008)
  - Websites:
    www.pbs.org/wnet/cryfromthegrave
    A timeline of events and statements from eyewitnesses

Pokémon Conquer the World

On 26 February 1996 a host of small monsters rushed out of Japan and colonized the whole world, taking over the minds of children. They did not loosen their grip for five years. Pokémon were a series of games and merchandising centring around fictional 'pocket monsters'. First released in February 1996 as a game for the Nintendo Game Boy, the characters soon appeared in comics, on trading cards, on TV, in books, in two feature films and on a host of merchandising.

Pokémon became the best-selling computer games and trading cards of all time. The trend encouraged a boom in trading card games, drove sales of handheld games consoles and brought Japanese anime to a worldwide audience.

An employee of Nintendo shows off the newly launched Pokémon game on the Game Boy Color Console.

Catch 'em all

In the Pokémon game, the player takes on the role of a trainer. He or she aims to collect Pokémon, small monsters of different species that hide in various environments. When a trainer meets a Pokémon, he or she throws a special ball to capture the monster. Captured Pokémon are pitted against others in battles, aiming either to capture them or absorb their strength. Experienced

What the media said

Kids are so eager to collect and trade the products ... that many schools, equally eager to keep their students' attention focused on learning, have declared themselves Pokémon-free zones.... Some parents ... worry that their children are falling into a dangerous world in which fantasy and reality become blurred.

CNN, 11 November 1999

When the Pokémon craze hit New York City, merchandising flooded the stores, along with the electronic games and trading cards.

Pokémon may 'evolve' into different, stronger forms. The aim is to collect all the different species and to train a team of powerful Pokémon. In the original game there were 151 Pokémon, but later releases added hundreds more.

Pokémon were invented by the Japanese games engineer Satoshi Tajiri. Inspired by his own love of collecting insects as a child, Tajiri developed the games to give other children the thrill of collecting creatures in a world where cities were largely paved and insects were hard to find.

Gameboys and cards

Pokémon was the first electronic game to appeal to girls and boys equally, and took computer gaming from the realm of geeky boys to a mainstream market. The Nintendo Game Boy, a small, handheld console with its own screen, was released in 1989. As the platform of the Pokémon games, it became the essential toy of the late 1990s. Three million copies of the first Pokémon game were sold in the first three months. But not all children could afford a Game Boy. Trading cards filled the gap, being easily affordable with pocket money. They were so popular that many schools banned them, saying they led to fights and distracted children from lessons. Newspapers even carried stories of children being bullied, robbed and cheated of their prized cards.

- **SEE ALSO**
  Pages 40–41: 8 July 1996
  The Spice Girls Release their First Hit

- **FURTHER INFORMATION**
  Websites:
  www.pokemon.com
  The original Pokémon website

Dolly the Sheep is Born

The birth of a sheep rarely attracts much news coverage. But Dolly was a very special sheep: she was the first mammal cloned from a cell taken from an adult animal. The scientific community was excited at the achievement and what it could mean for the future. Many people, though, worried that cloning was unnatural and that Dolly's birth might pave the way for developments they would find alarming, such as human cloning. Dolly went on to live a pampered life at the Roslin Institute in Scotland, where she was created, but died at the early age of six in 2003.

What the papers said

Now we know that we can clone an adult animal. And since what works in sheep is likely to be possible in humans, we are suddenly propelled right past the imagined techniques of Brave New World.... There are endless possibilities for futuristic speculation. The egotistical may be able to clone themselves and give themselves the upbringing that they always thought they deserved. The rich and powerful would be able to found dynasties where at death they would pass all their wealth to a genetically identical but younger version of themselves.

New Scientist, 1 March 1997

Making copies

A clone is a perfect copy of an animal or plant. Normally, an animal such as a sheep has two parents. Its DNA – the genetic material which acts as the 'recipe' for making it – comes from both parents. In a clone, all the DNA comes from one animal. In the case of Dolly, DNA was taken from a cell from the udder of an adult sheep. An egg cell was taken from a different adult sheep. The DNA was removed from the egg cell and all the DNA from the udder cell was put into it instead. The egg was then put into a third sheep to grow normally, being born as a baby sheep on 5 July 1996.

Unnatural interference?

When Dolly's birth was announced in January 1997, it caused some alarm. Many people argue that cloning is wrong, or fear that it is dangerous. Some worry that people may be cloned, or that babies will be started and used to 'harvest' human tissue for medical use. A South Korean group claimed to have created a human baby by cloning in 2002, but it turned out to be a lie. Cloning could be very useful, though. It could help to provide food for a hungry world by producing crops at a much faster rate. Cloning could also produce medicines or even body parts.

Dolly the cloned sheep stands in her stall at the Roslin Institute in Edinburgh. In 1996, Dolly became the first animal to be cloned from DNA taken from an adult animal.

Problems with cloning

Sheep often live 11 or 12 years, and some scientists think that the cloning process may have led to Dolly's early death. Many other cloned mammals have been created since Dolly, and early death and abnormalities are common. It is not clear yet whether these problems will always accompany cloning or whether the techniques currently used are to blame.

- **SEE ALSO**
Pages 4–5: 24 April 1990
The Hubble Space Telescope is Launched
Pages 20–21: 6 May 1994
The Channel Tunnel Opens

- **FURTHER INFORMATION**
  Books:
  Cloning and Genetic Engineering by Nicola Barber (Franklin Watts, 2013)
  Websites:
  www.sciencemuseum.org.uk/antenna/dolly/index.asp
  A profile of Dolly the sheep, and the implications of her life and death

Hong Kong Returns to China

Extravagant firework displays, dragon dances and parties marked the end of more than 100 years of British rule in Hong Kong as the island passed back to Chinese control. The celebrations even included a troupe of dancing children dressed as credit cards – a reference to Hong Kong's status as a thriving financial centre. In Beijing, 100,000 invited guests watched on giant television screens set up in Tiananmen Square.

The transfer ceremony took place at the Hong Kong Convention and Exhibition Centre moments before midnight on 30 June 1997. Before a crowd of 100,000, Prince Charles, the Prince of Wales, read a farewell speech, then the British and Hong Kong flags were removed and the Chinese flag raised. The last British governor of Hong Kong, Chris Patten, sobbed into his handkerchief. Chinese troops moved into Hong Kong immediately, but did nothing to stop the protests that took place in some parts of the island.

Britain's Prince Charles (centre), Chris Patten (3rd from right) and Prime Minister Tony Blair (2nd from right) at the Military Farewell Ceremony at the HMS Tamar military base in Hong Kong.

Waiting and worrying

Negotiations for the handover began in 1979. At that time, China was a harsh communist regime – a vast, poor nation strongly opposed to the free market economy that had made Hong Kong rich. The people and businesses of Hong Kong approached the handover with more anxiety than excitement.

Hong Kong is a bustling capitalist marketplace, one of the 'tiger economies' of Asia, along with Japan, Singapore, Taiwan and South Korea. Since 1945, these areas have grown rich making consumer goods

⊙ eye witness

If there is no democracy there will be no rule of law; if there is no freedom, human rights will not be respected.... We want the freedom we are entitled to under the Joint Declaration.

Martin Lee, leader of Hong Kong's Democratic Party

A spectacular dragon dance formed part of the celebrations at the handover of Hong Kong to China.

for the West. Many businesses with investments in Hong Kong feared they would suffer following its return to China.

One country, two systems

As the time for the handover approached, the Chinese leader Deng Xiaoping promised that China would be 'one country, two systems', with Hong Kong keeping its capitalist status for at least 50 years. This reassured some investors, but many moved out even so. Many Hong Kong residents feared that China would not honour the agreement to allow business in Hong Kong to continue.

To add to Hong Kong's concerns, China had a poor record on human rights, with harsh punishments and an unreliable justice system. After the Tiananmen Square massacre in 1989, when peaceful protestors were mown down by tanks and guns, the trickle of people leaving Hong Kong turned to a flood. Over a million people left, many going to Britain, the United States and Canada. But they need not have worried about Hong Kong's economic prospects. During the 1990s and 2000s, China's economy grew from strength to strength. It has opened up to foreign investment and trade, taken on board the capitalist business model, and is now a major economic power.

• **SEE ALSO**
Pages 12–13: 8 December 1991
The End of the Soviet Union
Pages 18–19: 27 April 1994
Black Rule in South Africa

• **FURTHER INFORMATION**
📖 Books:
China by Oliver James
(Franklin Watts, 2013)
🖱 Websites:
news.bbc.co.uk/news/world-asia-china-18662668
Hong Kong marks 15 years since the handover

The World Goes Green

On 11 December 1997, the world challenged climate change head on and began an international effort to avoid disaster. On that day, after two and a half years of negotiations, representatives of 150 countries drew up the Kyoto Protocol in Japan. The agreement set targets for reducing emissions of six greenhouse gases by 5 per cent of 1990 levels, by 2012.

The protocol built on the work of the Framework Convention on Climate Change of 1992. The convention encouraged countries to reduce their carbon emissions, whereas the protocol set out to force reductions. Developed countries were to reduce their greenhouse gas emissions immediately. Developing countries were to monitor and report emissions, but need not cut them. Each developed country had its own target for reducing emissions, tailored to its needs and capabilities. For example, the European Union overall were to reduce emissions by 8 per cent; Canada to cut emissions by 6 per cent.

Instead of reducing emissions, a country could find a partner for 'carbon trading'. By buying greenhouse gas allowance from a country that did not use all its allowance, a more extravagant country could continue to produce carbon emissions above its target.

What the papers said

Negotiators from more than 150 countries flew out of Kyoto, Japan, this week after agreeing only the weakest of compromises to combat global warming. A host of unresolved issues remain, each of which could yet make the agreement unworkable…. Some issues were left out of the deal altogether. These included emissions from aircraft and shipping, which make up as much as 5 per cent of global CO_2 [carbon dioxide – a greenhouse gas] emissions but remain outside any control agreement.

New Scientist, 13 December 1997

Climate change and carbon emissions

Global temperatures are rising, and this has begun to affect the natural world. Most scientists agree that the rise in greenhouse gases in the atmosphere is causing the temperature to rise, with potentially disastrous consequences for the world's population. Greenhouse gases are produced by burning fossil fuels such as coal, oil and gas and by intensive farming. Greenhouse gases trap the sun's heat within the atmosphere, thus raising global temperatures.

Young Japanese people protest against global warming in front of delegates to the UN conference on climate change in Kyoto.

In 1997 not everyone agreed that climate change was the result of human activities. Some countries used this doubt as a reason not to accept the agreement. The United States refused to sign the Kyoto Protocol, as did Australia. Politicians in these countries feared that cutting carbon emissions would damage trade and industry. They also wanted large developing countries to limit their own emissions. The United States withdrew completely from the discussions in 2001 after George W Bush became president.

After Kyoto

Kyoto was only the start. The agreement would not come into force until enough high-emitting countries had signed up to it. This target had been met by late 2004, and the Kyoto agreement came into force on 15 February 2005. In 2011, it was agreed to extend the Kyoto Protocol and to create a new, legally binding treaty in 2015.

• **FURTHER INFORMATION**

📖 Books:
Climate Change by Richard Spilsbury (Wayland, 2012)
In the News: Climate Change by Corona Brezina (ReadHowYouWant, 2012)

🖱 Websites:
www.epa.gov/climatechange/kids/index.html
A student's guide to climate change.

Massacre at Columbine High School

Students cowered under tables as two of their colleagues, Eric Harris and Dylan Klebold, sprayed them with bullets from automatic rifles. For nearly an hour the two killers rampaged through Columbine High School in Denver, USA, killing 13 people and injuring 24. Terrified students and staff tried to hide as the attackers began shooting outside, then moved into the cafeteria and finished with a massacre of students taking shelter under tables in the library. The gunmen shot themselves before police arrived. In addition to a range of guns, the killers used bombs of various types, many of which failed to detonate properly. At the time it was the third deadliest school massacre in US history.

Games and guns

The immediate public response in the United States was outrage. How could the boys have gathered so many weapons, made bombs, collected ammunition and planned their assault without anyone noticing? And what led them to kill their fellow school students?

Some people blamed the gun culture in the United States, saying that the ready availability of guns made it too easy for the killers to collect weapons. Others blamed violent computer games and videos for desensitizing the boys. Both students had been keen players of violent computer games. Harris had been banned from using the computer at home as a punishment for bad behaviour. Some people thought he turned to violence when he could not express his anger and frustration in a game.

Pupils at Columbine High School comfort each other following the massacre.

Harris and Klebold had previously been arrested for stealing weapons. Harris posted entries on his blog listing the guns he had and the people he wanted to kill. He then made threats of violence towards students and staff at the school. Although the police knew about the website, they took no action.

Other school massacres

School massacres are rare outside the United States. Britain's only school massacre was in Dunblane, Scotland. On 13 March 1996 Thomas Hamilton killed 15 children and a teacher in Dunblane primary school. Hamilton was not killing fellow students, though. He was an adult with no direct connection with the school he targeted. In 1993 a gunman took six children and an adult hostage in a nursery school in Paris, France, and demanded a ransom of US$18.5 million.

This is a still from a home video made some six weeks before the massacre. It shows Eric Harris (left) and Dylan Klebold at a makeshift shooting range in Douglas County, Colorado.

What the papers said

So the violence is over. Innocents are dead. The perpetrators are dead. The survivors are scarred. The rest of us wonder why. Is the ever-ready limelight of news coverage creating a self-replicating youth trend – massacre chic?... But one eyewitness account seems to drive home the futility of reasoned solutions. 'They were laughing after they shot,' said Columbine student Aaron Cohn. 'It was like they were having the time of their life.' And they were. No solution to *that*, except to wait for the next time, and hope it never comes.

Time, 21 April 1999

- **SEE ALSO**
  Pages 22–23: 20 March 1995
  Nerve Gas Attack on the Tokyo Underground
  Pages 26–27: 12 July 1995
  Massacre at Srebrenica

- **FURTHER INFORMATION**
  Books:
  The Columbine School Shootings
  by Louise I Gerdes (Greenhaven Press, 2012)
  Movies:
  Bowling for Columbine written and directed
  by Michael Moore (2002)

Millennium Fever

Around the world, firework displays, free concerts and massive public parties marked the end of the millennium at midnight on 31 December 1999. Celebrations took place in a wave as midnight arrived at different places around the world, beginning with the uninhabited Millennium Island in the middle of the Pacific. Sunrise on Millennium Island on 1 January 2000 was televized around the world.

Party like it's 1999

Many countries built lasting structures, such as bridges, pavilions, sports stadia and parks to mark the new millennium. There were also many temporary structures and exhibitions, such as the Millennium Exhibition in the Millennium Dome in London and La Grande Roue, a large ferris wheel in La Place de la Concorde in Paris, France.

Although the new millennium was celebrated on 1 January 2000, many people argued that it would actually start in 2001. As the calendar has no 'year 0', the first millennium was 1–1000, the second millennium 1001–2000.

The millennium bug

While most people celebrated, many worried that computer programs would go wrong, perhaps with catastrophic results, or that terrorists would try to attack. A few religious groups even believed the world would come to an end.

Many computer programs written during the 1980s and earlier had no way of storing a year for the date that contained more than two digits. So the year 1995, for instance, would be shown as '95'. At the start of the year 2000, the year would be stored as '00' and the computer would assume it meant 1900. Experts warned that if the problem was not fixed, planes might

What the papers said

Two thousand years after Christ's obscure birth in a dusty town in Judea, the world's six billion people ... rode their turning blue planet across time's invisible line today and, by common consent, looked into the dawn of a new millennium.... What they saw first was a party. It was garish, glittering and global, and millions, setting religious considerations and personal concerns aside, joined in the festivities to celebrate the conjunction of a new year, a new century and a new thousand-year cycle of history. They also put aside the inconvenient fact that the millennium, technically, is still a year off.

New York Times, 1 January 2000

Christians celebrate the millennium in front of the Church of the Nativity in Bethlehem, the city traditionally regarded as the birthplace of Jesus.

fall out of the sky (since their systems would register that they had not yet taken off), power stations would fail and untold numbers of computer-controlled processes would stop or go wrong. The potential for disaster seemed huge.

Around the world, organizations and governments invested billions of dollars in converting all their computer programs to recognize four-digit dates, so that '2000' clearly came after '1999'. As the hour of midnight approached on 31 December 1999, the world held its breath. In fact, there were very few problems. This may have been because of the actions taken, or the problem might have been overstated – it will never be clear.

• **FURTHER INFORMATION**

📖 **Books:**
The Time Book: A Brief History from Lunar Calendars to Atomic Clocks by Martin Jenkins (Walker, 2010)

🖱 **Websites:**
http://news.bbc.co.uk/onthisday/hi/dates/stories/january/1/newsid_2478000/2478173.stm
A BBC report on the first day of the new millennium.

The Spice Girls Release their First Hit

Yo, I'll tell you what I want, what I really really want,
So tell me what you want, what you really really want,
I'll tell you what I want, what I really really want...

The release of 'Wannabe', the first single by the Spice Girls, marked a new departure in British pop music. The build-up to the single's release had been massive, an expertly managed publicity drive designed to raise expectations to fever pitch. The single entered the British charts at number 3, reaching number 1 the following week and staying there for the next seven weeks. It was the most successful debut single ever and the best-selling single by a girl band of all time, selling 4 million copies and reaching number 1 in 31 countries. It had taken less than an hour to record the song.

The Spice Girls. Clockwise from top left, they are: Scary Spice, Sporty Spice, Baby Spice, Posh Spice and Ginger Spice.

Putting it together

The all-girl band of five had been put together by a music management company hoping to match the success of boy bands such as Take That and New Kids on the Block. The final line-up was Geri Haliwell, Victoria Adams, Melanie Chisholm ('Mel C'), Emma Bunton and Melanie Brown ('Mel B').

Soon the girls broke with the original plan, exercising the 'girl power' their songs promoted. They stole their demo tapes, found a new manager and changed their name from Touch to the Spice Girls. Their nicknames – Posh, Baby, Scary, Sporty and Ginger – were invented by an editorial team at *Top of the Pops* magazine just before the first single came out.

The Spice Girls' themes, female empowerment and the importance of friendship, quickly became a hit with young girls. They had four consecutive number one hits (the first band in history to do so), five other number ones, and a successful film, *Spiceworld*.

Image conscious

The Spice Girls were part of the 'Britpop' phenomenon – the wave of young British pop bands in the mid-1990s that included Blur, Oasis, Pulp and the Verve. Britpop was itself part of a larger British cultural movement known as 'Cool Britannia'. The term Cool Britannia started as the name of a Ben & Jerry's ice cream flavour, but soon came to stand for the lively, optimistic and patriotic attitude of young British artists, musicians and fashion designers. The Union Jack dress worn by Geri Halliwell was an icon of this movement.

Geri Halliwell (Ginger Spice) on stage at the Brit Awards, in her famous Union Jack dress.

Time to split

In 1999, Geri Halliwell left the Spice Girls. In 2000, the group changed its musical style and sales dropped. The girls began to pursue solo careers and in 2001 they decided to split up. When the Spice Girls reformed in 2007 for a comeback world tour, tickets for the first London gig sold out in 38 seconds. But it didn't work out, and the tour was cut short. They reformed once again to perform at the closing ceremony of the 2012 London Olympics.

What the papers said

Just when boys with guitars threaten to rule pop life, an all-girl, in-yer-face pop group has arrived with enough sass to burst that rockist cherry!!

Paul Gorman, *Music Week*

- **SEE ALSO**
  Pages 28–29: 26 February 1996
  Pokémon Conquer the World

- **FURTHER INFORMATION**
- Books:
  Alternative, Country, Hip-Hop, Rap and More: Music from the 1980s to Today by Michael Ray (Rosen Education Service, 2012)
- Websites:
  www.thespicegirls.com
  Official Spice Girls website

Princess Diana Dies

Throughout the UK, people were shocked and stunned by the news of the sudden death of their favourite royal, Diana, Princess of Wales, on 31 August 1997. The princess and her partner Dodi Al-Fayed were both killed in a car crash in Paris, France.

After dinner at the Ritz Hotel, the couple left by a back door and headed to the Al-Fayeds' private villa. The driver raced ahead of a pack of photographers, speeding into the Pont de l'Alma Tunnel under the River Seine. Driving at 90–110 kilometres per hour, he lost control while trying to avoid another car and crashed into a concrete post. The driver and Dodi were killed immediately. Diana died in hospital, and her bodyguard was seriously injured. The extravagant public display of grief lasted for weeks. More than a million people lined the streets to watch the funeral cortege take the princess's coffin to Westminster Abbey for her funeral. Around the country, people signed books of condolence, sharing their thoughts and memories of her. Tens of thousands of people queued outside Kensington Palace, the princess's home, to sign a book of condolence. The palace stayed open 24 hours a day until everyone had signed. Many cities and towns named parks, buildings or gardens after her. The princess was buried on an island at her childhood home, Althorpe, in Northampton.

The wreckage of the Mercedes Benz car in which Princess Diana and her companion Dodi Al-Fayed died following a crash in Paris.

eye witness

It was an extraordinary time for absolutely everyone working in the palace. You really felt you had become caught up in a little bit of the history of this nation.

Joanna Marschner, curator of Kensington Palace in 1997

Princess Diana meets victims of landmines at a rehabilitation centre in Huambo, Angola. Diana worked extensively to help landmine victims and to outlaw the use of landmines.

A fairytale turned sour

Diana had married Charles, Prince of Wales, in 1981. Popular with the public from the start, she was soon dubbed 'the people's princess' by the media. The public had watched her evolve from a plump nursery school teacher into an elegant and beautiful public figure. Her involvement with charitable causes, such as children with Aids and landmine victims, made her even more popular. But privately, the princess suffered eating disorders and pain from her troubled marriage. She and Charles divorced in 1996.

Looking for causes

The cool response to her death from the British Royal Family damaged the image of the monarchy and added to rumours of a conspiracy to kill the princess. The father of Dodi Al-Fayed, the Egyptian businessman Mohamed Al-Fayed, who owned the London department store Harrods, was one of the first to claim the couple had been killed deliberately. Two inquiries (2004–2006 and 2007–2008) found no evidence of a conspiracy.

The press photographers who pursued the car were criticized, but none of them were prosecuted. The code of conduct governing what photographers may do was tightened in December 1997. Although the British media have taken a more careful approach towards the Royal Family since, Diana's son Prince Harry had to return early from active military service in Afghanistan in 2008 after foreign press had revealed his whereabouts.

- **FURTHER INFORMATION**
- **Books:**
  Diana: The People's Princess
  by Lisa Owings (Essential Library, 2012)
- **Websites:**
  www.cnn.co.uk/CNN/Programs/people/shows/
  diana/profile.html
  Profile of Princess Diana

Good Friday Agreement

After 30 years of violence, the Belfast Agreement brought a solution to the Troubles in Northern Ireland on Good Friday 1998. It soon became known as the Good Friday Agreement. The agreement gave Northern Ireland its own elected parliament, independent of the British parliament. Under the agreement, violent paramilitary groups agreed to give up their weapons and the Republic of Ireland gave up its claim to Northern Ireland.

A long history of problems

Since 1921, Ireland has been divided in two. Northern Ireland, where most of the population are Protestant, is part of the UK. The south is the independent Republic of Ireland. Here, most of the population are Catholic. The Northern Ireland government, Stormont, discriminated against Catholics in Northern Ireland for most of the 20th century. The larger Protestant community enjoyed better jobs and housing. The Royal Ulster Constabulary (RUC – the police force of Northern Ireland) followed the lead of Stormont and also favoured the Protestant community.

British prime minister Tony Blair (right) and Irish prime minister Bertie Ahern shake hands following the signing of the Good Friday Agreement.

The Troubles

Tensions between the Protestant and Catholic communities flared into violence in 1968. The conflict, known as the Troubles, would last for the next 30 years. In 1969, the British government sent in troops to try to keep the peace, but their heavy-handed response further angered Catholics. The Provisional IRA was a paramilitary organization that wanted Northern and southern Ireland to be united. They began carrying out terrorist attacks on army and civilian targets both in Northern Ireland and the British mainland. Meanwhile, loyalist (Protestant) paramilitary groups attacked the Catholic community.

The search for peace

The British and Irish governments and parties within Northern Ireland tried to start peace talks several times during the Troubles. The talks leading to the Good Friday agreement made progress where others had failed for a number of reasons. Firstly, during the late 1980s and early 1990s, the Northern Ireland government introduced new laws to end discrimination against Catholics. Secondly, many republicans (supporters of a united Ireland) turned away from violence and tried to achieve their aims by peaceful political means. Finally, a new generation of politicians brought a fresh approach to the problem. Two of the key figures in the peace talks, David Trimble and John Hume, shared the Nobel Prize for Peace in 1998 for their part in the Good Friday Agreement.

Four months after the signing of the Good Friday Agreement, a group calling itself the Real IRA detonated a car bomb in Omagh, Northern Ireland, killing 29. Condemned by all sides, the attack helped to spur on the peace process.

After Good Friday

The Good Friday Agreement was approved in a referendum, but it did not bring peace immediately. A new government was established, the Northern Ireland Assembly, based on the Protestant and Catholic communities sharing power. However, it was suspended several times because unionists (Protestants) were angry that the IRA did not disarm more quickly. From 2002, Northern Ireland returned to direct rule by the UK. Finally, in 2007, a further agreement was signed and Northern Ireland was once more given control of its own affairs.

eye witness

Violent republicanism has failed to 'smash the Union'; in fact it has failed in all its stated objectives. Instead, Northern Ireland's place within the United Kingdom has been secured; the Act of Union ... remains firmly in place; ... a Northern Ireland Assembly will be established; ... and the South now accepts the legitimacy of Northern Ireland.

David Trimble, 17 April 1998

- **SEE ALSO**
  Pages 18–19: 27 April 1994
  Black Rule in South Africa
  Pages 32–33: 1 July 1997
  Hong Kong Returns to China

- **FURTHER INFORMATION**
- Books:
  The Troubles in Northern Ireland
  by Tony Allen
  (Heinemann, 2005)
- Websites:
  http://news.bbc.co.uk/1/hi/northern_ireland
  /4079267.stm
  The Good Friday agreement

People of the Decade

Aung San Suu Kyi
(1945–)
Aung San Suu Kyi is leader of the National League for Democracy in Burma. She leads a peaceful, non-violent struggle against the military dictatorship in Burma. She was placed repeatedly under house arrest between 1989 and 2010. Upon her release, she vowed to continue her opposition to military rule. Suu Kyi is considered by the National League for Democracy to be the legitimate prime minister of Burma. She won the Nobel Prize for Peace in 1991.

Bill Clinton
(1946–)
Bill Clinton was 42nd president of the United States, in office 1993–2001. Although his presidency was marred by scandals and indictment for perjury (of which he was cleared), he retained international popularity. He presided over the longest period of peacetime economic growth in the United States since 1945 and made substantial efforts to broker peace in the Middle East. His policies at home included improving the education system, healthcare provision and job prospects. Internationally, he authorized the use of US troops as part of a NATO force in Yugoslavia.

Kurt Cobain
(1967–1994)
American guitarist, singer and songwriter Kurt Cobain co-founded the iconic alternative band Nirvana in 1987. Nirvana was hugely successful, bringing to the fore the music of the Seattle 'grunge' scene. Cobain suffered from bronchitis and stomach pains all his life, and became addicted to heroin, which he claimed eased his physical pain. He killed himself in 1994. By this time, Nirvana had become one of the most popular and influential bands of the era.

Bill Gates
(1955–)
Bill Gates is an American businessman and computer pioneer and one of the richest people in the world. He established the computer company Microsoft in 1975. Gates produced the operating system DOS used by IBM PCs and in 1985 Microsoft launched the first version of Windows. Microsoft went on to dominate the software industry with its main products, Windows and Microsoft Office, used worldwide. Gates has given billions of dollars for charitable causes through the foundations he has set up.

Saddam Hussein
(1937–2006)
Saddam Hussein was president of Iraq 1979–2003. He created a repressive security force that gave him a powerful hold on the country. During the 1990s his invasion of Kuwait, attacks on his own people and refusal to cooperate with UN weapons inspectors made him an enemy of the West, and especially of the United States. He was deposed in 2003 following an invasion of Iraq by a US-led coalition. He was convicted of illegally killing Shi'ite opponents and executed in 2006.

Helmut Kohl
(1930–)
Helmut Kohl was chancellor of Germany from 1982 to 1998. As one of the most influential European politicians of the second half of the 20th century, he oversaw the reunification of Germany in 1990. Kohl worked with President François Mitterand of France to push through the Maastricht Treaty (1992), which created the European Union. He was also instrumental in the introduction of the Euro, the European currency now used in 17 member states.

Nelson Mandela
(1918–)
Nelson Mandela became the first black president of South Africa following the country's first fully democratic elections in 1994. He was active in the anti-apartheid movement of the African National Congress (ANC) from 1952. In 1962 he was arrested and imprisoned for 27 years. He gained international support as the figurehead of the the anti-apartheid cause, which he continued to champion from prison. He was released from prison in 1990 and won the Nobel Prize for Peace in 1993.

J K Rowling
(1965–)
British writer Joanne Rowling is the author of the 'Harry Potter' novels, which took the publishing world by storm in the 1990s. Rowling became the best-selling children's novelist of all time, with all seven of the books in the series topping the bestseller charts and titles four to seven breaking sales records on their release. The Potter novels built a substantial following, further increased by the release of the films of the books from 2001. She published her first adult novel, *The Casual Vacancy*, in 2012.

Boris Yeltsin
(1931–2007)
The first president of the Russian Federation, 1991–1999, Yeltsin promised reforms that would bring economic renewal to Russia. However, his attempts at turning the ex-communist state into a free market economy failed dismally. Privatization and free pricing enabled a handful of businesspeople to enrich themselves while leaving vast numbers in poverty. Corruption and violent crime were rife in Yeltsin's Russia, and on several occasions the country teetered on the brink of economic collapse.

Glossary

capitalist A system in which trade and industry are controlled by private owners for profit.

coalition Two or more political parties that have agreed to work together.

communist A system, or the belief in a system, in which capitalism is overthrown and the state controls wealth and property.

condolence An expression of sympathy with someone's grief.

confederation A group of states acting together.

conspiracy A secret plan by several people or organizations to do something illegal or underhand.

cortege People and vehicles making up a funeral procession.

democracy A system of government in which the leaders have been elected freely and equally by all the citizens of a country, or a country with such a system.

detonate Set off an explosive device.

dormant Inactive.

economic sanctions Financial methods of making a rogue state comply with the wishes of other states, including refusing to trade or imposing high taxes on the state's exports.

emissions Gases released as a product of natural or human activity.

eruption (volcanic) The rapid outpouring of hot gases, ash and lava from a volcano.

forensic Relating to the investigation of crime by examining physical evidence in detail, often using scientific methods.

free market economy An economic system in which the price of goods and services is allowed to find its own level as dictated by supply and demand.

genocide The killing of, or the attempt to kill, a whole race of people.

greenhouse gases Carbon gases that help to trap heat near the earth, causing the planet to warm up.

Holocaust The Nazis' genocidal campaign (1942–1945) to exterminate Jews and some other groups.

humanitarian Describing something done benevolently, in the interests of humankind.

indictment A formal charge of having committed a crime.

mafia A very large, organized criminal gang.

mandate An official authorization to rule.

merchandising Consumer goods licensed with a brand or character.

nationalist Supportive of the right of one's people to exist as a nation, or belief in the status of one's nation above all others.

Ottoman Empire An empire under the control of Turkey until the end of World War I.

paramilitary Describing an organization that uses a military structure, weapons and tactics and fights within a country, usually against the government.

perjury The crime of lying under oath in court.

protocol A formal agreement between nations.

puppet regime A government installed and under the control of an external power.

rabies A viral infection of animals that can be passed on to humans and is usually fatal. Rabies affects the nervous system.

reconciliation The ending of a conflict or renewal of friendly relations between people, groups or countries.

red giant A star in the late stages of its life when it grows very large and glows red.

referendum A vote by the whole of an electorate on a particular question put to it by a government.

refugee A person who has fled from their home because of a natural disaster, war or other catastrophe.

republic A state with a form of government in which supreme power is in the hands of representatives elected by the people.

sarin An extremely poisonous gas that attacks the central nervous system, causing convulsions and death.

sect A small, close-knit group with strongly held views, sometimes viewed as extreme by most people.

sediment Solid matter deposited by or in a liquid.

shanty town A settlement of rough, often temporary, buildings or huts inhabited by very poor people.

Soviet Union Also known as the USSR, a country consisting of Russia and a number of other East European, Baltic and Central Asian countries. The Soviet Union existed from 1922 to 1991.

tiger economy Any of several states in South-East Asia that underwent rapid economic growth during the second half of the 20th century.

township In apartheid South Africa, townships were urban settlements planned for black people only, usually with inferior facilities and services.

toxin Poison.

tsar A ruler of the Russian Empire.

Index

Page numbers in **bold** refer to illustrations